NUTTALL, Gina

Puppets around the world

D0996254

Puppets Around the World

Gina Nuttall

QED Publishing

First published in the UK in 2004 by
QED Publishing
A division of Quarto Publishing plc
The Fitzpatrick Building
188–194 York Way, London N7 9QP

A Catalogue record for this book is available from the British Library.

ISBN 1 84538 018 5

Written by Gina Nuttall
Designed by Zeta Jones
Editor Hannah Ray
Picture Researcher Joanne Beardwell
Photographer Michael Wicks p20–21

Series Consultant Anne Faundez
Creative Director Louise Morley
Editorial Manager Jean Coppendale

Printed and bound in China

Picture credits
Key: t = top, b = bottom, m = middle, c = centre, l = left, r = right

Christies Images 9t, 22t; **Corbis**/Bettmann Corbis 18, 19, 22mr, 22bl /Michael
Freeman 5m, /Historical Picture Archive 10t, /Arne Hodalic 10b, /Bob Krist 4–5,
22ml/ Chris North 15b, 22br, /Reza Webistan 11 /Nick Wheeler 16–17, /Adam
Woolfitt 14, 22tr /Michael S Yamashita 12–13, 22tl; **Getty Images**/Colin
Hawkins 15t; **Musee Gadagne** 8t, 9b; **Panos Pictures**/Dermot Tatlow 6–7.

Contents

A world of puppets

People all around the world make and use puppets.

Puppets come in many different sizes and forms.

Puppets can be silly and funny.

Puppets can be beautiful and magical.

People have used puppets for a long, long time to:
• tell stories
• entertain people
• teach lessons

China

Marionette puppets are very popular in China.

People celebrate special days and events with puppet shows.

Strings are attached to the head, hands and legs of the puppets. The strings are attached to a wooden rod. The **puppeteer** moves the rod to make the puppet work. He works the puppet from above. The audience cannot see him.

7

France

France has a famous puppet called Guignol.

Guignol is a hand puppet. He has a wooden or papier-mâché head.

Guignol was invented in 1808. There was a man who pulled out people's bad teeth. He wanted more people to come to him. So he put on puppet shows. Guignol the puppet helped him to get more customers!

Guignol and his puppet friends talk to people about important things that are happening in the town.

Guignol has a girlfriend. Her name is Madelon.

Guignol's best friend is called Gnafron.

Indonesia

In Indonesia, shadow puppets often tell Hindu stories.

The puppets are flat, like paper dolls. They have arms and legs that move.

The puppets are sometimes made of leather.

10

Rods are used to work the puppets.

The puppeteer stands behind a screen.

A light shines on the screen from behind.

The people watch the shadows of the puppets on the screen.

Japan

The story is so exciting that the audience forgets that they can see the puppeteers!

Japan has a very special type of puppet show called **bunraku**.

Japanese bunraku puppets are big. They can be 1.5 metres high!

Bunraku puppets are made of wood. The head, the body, each arm and leg are all different parts.

The puppeteers wear black clothes, but the audience can see them as they work the puppets.

Britain

Most children in Britain know about the Punch and Judy puppet shows.

They can often see them at the seaside.

Punch is the only puppet in the show with legs.

The puppet shows are very funny.

Punch speaks in a very squeaky voice.

He is married to Judy. They are always fighting and fooling about.

The puppets are hand or glove puppets.

The puppeteer stands inside a folding **booth**.

Vietnam

16

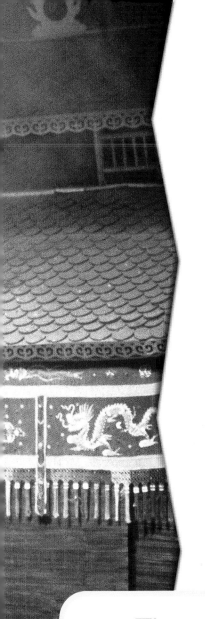

These puppets from Vietnam are very unusual. They perform on water!

The puppeteers stand behind the green screen in the water. They use hidden strings and bamboo rods to move the puppets. The puppets seem to come from under the water!

The puppets are made from wood. Then they are painted to make them waterproof.

The puppets tell stories from Vietnamese myths and legends.

Charlie is a famous **dummy**!

Edgar is his puppeteer.
He is called a **ventriloquist**.

Dummies are about the same size as a small child.

A dummy puppet sits on the puppeteer's lap.

18

Charlie McCarthy

EDGAR BERGEN

Dummies' mouths can open and close. This makes them look like they are speaking and showing feelings.

The puppeteer speaks for the puppet, but does not move his lips. It is like magic!

Make your own puppet

What you need

- Felt
- Ruler
- Scissors
- Glue
- A collection of art materials for decoration: e.g. scraps of material, buttons, marker pens, knitting wool.

A finger puppet fits on one finger. You can make one for each finger.

1. Use a ruler to measure out two rectangles of felt: 4.5cm x 8cm.

2. Cut out the rectangles.

3. Glue the edges of the two rectangles together. Leave the bottom end open for your finger.

4. Let the glue dry. Use scissors to round off the corners of the head.

5. Decide what character you want your puppet to be. It could be an animal, a person or even a monster! Now use the other materials to make eyes, a nose, a mouth, ears, hair and so on.

Glossary

 **booth** – a moveable stage for puppets.

 **bunraku** – (pronounced bun-rah-koo) a type of Japanese puppet show using large puppets.

 **dummy** – a life-like wooden lap puppet.

Charlie McCarthy

 **marionette** – a string puppet.

 **puppeteer** – a person who works a puppet.

 **ventriloquist** – (pronounced ven-tril-o-kwist) a puppeteer who makes his/her voice seem to come from a dummy.

Index

Carers' and teachers' notes

- Talk with your child about the purpose of a glossary (tells the reader the meaning of words related to the subject of the text) and an index (tells the reader on which page to look to find something). Both are in alphabetical order. Play a quiz game with your child based on information in the glossary and index (e.g. 'What is a marionette?' 'Which pages would you look at to find out about shadow puppets?')
- Together, find the places mentioned in the book on a globe or in an atlas.
- Use the instructions on pages 20–21 to make some finger puppets with your child.
- Make up a play for the finger puppets. Then help your child to write it as a playscript.
- Use your child's own puppets to talk to them about issues that might be concerning them.
- Find out how to make another kind of puppet, e.g. a glove puppet – and help your child to make one. Before you start, ask your child to say what he/she will need in order to make the puppet, and to choose appropriate materials and implements.

- Encourage your child to use the instructions on page 20–21 as a model for writing instructions explaining how to make the new puppet.
- Together, use the Internet or books from the library to find out about other kinds of puppets, such as paper-bag puppets, or famous puppets such as Pinocchio.
- Encourage your child to make his/her own 'Puppets' book. On each page, ask your child to draw a picture of a different kind of puppet. Together, write a sentence or label to explain each picture.
- Talk about how puppets can show feelings, for example, some have moveable facial features. If they do not, the puppeteer needs to show a puppet's feelings by the way it moves and speaks, and by what it says.
- Watch a television programme that features puppets. Having read this book, can your child tell you what sort of puppets they are?
- Ask your child to pretend that he/she is a marionette. Pretend to move his/her strings. Make up some speech to go with your child's actions.